A FAITHFUL CHURCH MEMBER

A FAITHFUL CHURCH MEMBER

Joel R. Beeke

PUBLISHING WITH A MISSION

EP BOOKS
Faverdale North, Darlington, DL3 0PH, England

e-mail: sales@epbooks.org
web: http://www.epbooks.org

133 North Hanover Street
Carlisle, PA 17013, USA

e-mail: usasales@epbooks.org
web: http://www.epbooks.us

First published 2011

British Library Cataloguing in Publication Data available

ISBN-13: 978-0-85234-777-5
ISBN-10: 0-85234-777-4

Unless otherwise indicated, all Scripture quotations are from the Holy Bible, Authorized (King James) Version.

Printed and bound in the USA.

CONTENTS

He that descended is the same also that ascended up far above all heavens, that he might fill all things. And he gave some, apostles; and some, prophets; and some, evangelists; and some, pastors and teachers; for the perfecting of the saints, for the work of the ministry, for the edifying of the body of Christ: till we all come in the unity of the faith, and of the knowledge of the Son of God, unto a perfect man, unto the measure of the stature of the fulness of Christ: that we henceforth be no more children, tossed to and fro, and carried about with every wind of doctrine, by the sleight of men, and cunning craftiness, whereby they lie in wait to deceive; but speaking the truth in love, may grow up into him in all things, which is the head, even Christ: from whom the whole body fitly joined together and compacted by that which every joint supplieth, according to the effectual working in the measure of every part, maketh increase of the body unto the edifying of itself in love

(Ephesians 4:10–16).

THE PROBLEM

For an annual fee, you can be a member of your community recreational centre, where you have access to its exercise equipment and swimming pool. If you choose never to visit the building, it's no problem. You can sit at home and eat ice cream all day and never get your membership revoked. So long as you pay your dues, you are a member.

Similarly, you can be a member of a book club or a music club that offers great deals on books or CDs. Club mailings say you are under no obligation to buy anything; you can return a book or CD at any time and cancel your membership.

In such a cultural setting, it is not surprising that membership in a local church has also become non-demanding. One denomination discovered that, on average, only 70 of its 233 members attended church worship.[1] The church leadership is partly responsible for this easy membership by not upholding biblical standards and discipline. So are people's views of the church. Some people treat the church like a museum that preserves memories and artefacts from the past, to be revisited from time to time. Others go to church as if it were a shopping mall, where they seek programmes and services that will meet their own needs or those of their family.

Perhaps in reaction to this shopping-mall image, some people have redefined the church as a community outreach programme. Some groups occasionally cancel Sunday worship services to rake leaves, wash cars, distribute food to needy people, or have a picnic in a nearby park. Worshipping God on the Lord's Day is replaced by social service programmes, missionary outreach, or recreation and entertainment.

To correct a faulty view of the church, we must go back to the biblical concept of the church. The Bible tells us the church is the body of Christ. A Christian, then, is a living part of a larger body of people. That is the essence of Ephesians 4:10-16, which says the church is a living organism. It is a spiritual and relational body; each Christian is a member, much as a hand or foot is a body part. Christ is the Head of this body. He and all his members are bound together by the Holy Spirit and the bond of true faith. That is amazing because Christ is the Son of God, and we are fallen human beings. It is also amazing because Christians in the church are so different from each other; they are Jews and Gentiles, men and women of all countries and ethnicities, old and young, rich and poor. These diverse people are nonetheless bound together all over the world as a living organism of which Christ is the Head.

This truth has profound implications for what it means to be a member of the church of Jesus Christ. Paul reminds us in Ephesians 4:10-16 that membership in the church is all about Christ. We will focus our attention on five areas of marks: Christ's Word, his person, his people, his cause and his image. We will examine what it means to be a faithful member of the body of Christ in each of these areas in the (1) personal, (2) public, and (3) practical dimensions of our lives. Thus, we will take a look at fifteen characteristics of a faithful church member.

MARK ONE:
RECEIVING CHRIST'S WORD

Ephesians 4:11-13 tells us that Christ gives pastors and teachers to the church to the end that 'we all come in the unity of the faith, and of the knowledge of the Son of God, unto a perfect man, unto the measure of the stature of the fulness of Christ'. Christ has ascended far above the heavens to give gifts to the church so that his glory will fill the earth. In his glorified state, Christ extends his kingdom by giving servants of the Word to his church. His goal is to bring his elect together in Christ-centred faith and knowledge.

The primary tool the Carpenter-King uses to build the House of God is his Word, first of all as taught by the pastors and teachers of his church. Therefore, the first mark of a faithful church member is *receiving Christ's Word* — not merely as an individual reading his Bible at home but also as a church member listening to the Word proclaimed by the pastors and teachers of a local church and applying it to his life. Specifically, receiving Christ's Word involves the following:

Personal hunger for the Word

In 1 Peter 2:2, the apostle Peter urges all Christians to thirst for the sincere milk of the Word, 'that ye may grow thereby'. If you are sick and have no appetite, you feel only nausea when served a delicious meal. The longer supper lasts, the more restless you become. Some people experience the preaching of the Word like that: a sermon makes them uncomfortable. They blame a minister for preaching too long, but the problem is that they have no hunger for the Word. How different is the person who comes to the table with a full appetite! Even a simple meal of meat and potatoes is a feast to someone who is hungry. So it is with a person who has a healthy appetite for the preaching of the Word.

Faithful attendance at corporate worship

Hunger for the Word in church is expressed publicly by faithful attendance at church worship services.

Hebrews 10:25 says we must not forsake assembling ourselves in corporate worship. Christian worship fills us with the Word. Colossians 3:16 says, 'Let the word of Christ dwell in you richly in all wisdom; teaching and admonishing one another in psalms and hymns and spiritual songs, singing with grace in your hearts to the Lord.' Charles Spurgeon (1834–1892) wrote: 'There is no worship of God that is better than hearing of a sermon … it stirs all the coals of fire in your spirit, and makes them burn with a brighter flame.'[2]

Active listening to the Word

Jesus describes four kinds of listeners to the Word in the parable of the soils, only one of which receives the Word, perseveres in faith, and goes on to bear abundant fruit. In Luke 8:18a, Jesus says, 'Take heed therefore how ye hear.' On Saturday, prepare for Sabbath worship by asking God to open his Word to you and to open your heart to his Word. As you go to church, remind yourself that you are going to the throne of God to hear him speak. John Calvin (1509–1564) wrote: 'Whenever the gospel is preached, it is as if God himself came into the midst of us.'[3] What an awesome thought! When you sit before a preacher, stir up your mind to listen actively, as one who hears the living voice of God.

A grown man or woman would be ashamed of being spoon-fed from a jar of baby food, yet how many Christians expect a minister to spoon-feed them the Word! Cut your food and chew it for yourself. Think about what the preacher is saying. Train your soul like an athlete who disciplines his body by hard exercise to be stronger, faster and more skilful. Take notes on the sermon, giving special attention to the main points, Scripture references and personal applications. Listen with humble self-examination. Listen with delight to the words of life.

Thomas Watson (*c.* 1620–1686) offered numerous directives on how to actively listen to the preaching of the Word, such as, by coming to the Word with a holy appetite and a teachable heart; by sitting attentively under the Word, receiving it with meekness, and mingling it with faith. We can help ourselves to retain the Word by praying over it, practising it, and speaking to others about it. 'Dreadful is the case of those who go loaded with sermons to hell,' said Watson.[4]

Ephesians 4:10-14 says the exalted Christ builds up his church through his Word. The risen Christ gave the gifts of apostles, prophets, evangelists, pastors and teachers, all servants of the Word, to the church. Therefore we as members of that church must be faithful in receiving and seeking to profit by their ministry of the Word.

BIBLE STUDY QUESTIONS

1. *Personal hunger for the Word*: Read 1 Peter 2:1-3. If a baby has little appetite for milk, we grow very concerned. What does it tell us if a person professing to be a Christian shows little appetite for biblical preaching? What causes for this lack of spiritual appetite are suggested by verses 1 and 3? What would be its cure?

2. *Faithful attendance at corporate worship*: Read Hebrews 10:19-25. Christians are people who draw near to the holy God through Christ our Priest. According to verse 25, what is an essential part of drawing near to God? Why is that essential to drawing near to God?

3. *Active listening to the Word*: Read Luke 8:11-15, 18. In light of the parable of the soils, what are the dangers we face when hearing the preaching of the Word? How can we resist these dangers and become better listeners?

Mark Two:
Union with Christ's person

Christ gives his Word to call us into union with him (Rom. 1:6; 2 Thess. 2:14). In Ephesians 4:15-16, Paul commands the saints of God to grow into Christ in all things. Christ is the Head of his body; all our growth, which lifts us into closer communion with him, comes from him. Therefore, one must be a member of Christ to be a member of the body of Christ. Paul says in 1 Corinthians 6:15, 17, 'Know ye not that your bodies are the members of Christ? … he that is joined unto the Lord is one spirit.' A faithful relationship with the church grows out of a faithful relationship with the Lord Jesus. The mark of a true member of the church is not merely what he or she does for the church. It is a faithful response to Paul's challenge in 2 Corinthians 13:5: 'Examine yourselves, whether ye be in the faith; prove your own selves. Know ye not your own selves, how that Jesus Christ is in you, except ye be reprobates?' You are not truly in the church until Christ is truly in you.

Personally trusting in Christ

Colossians 2:6-7 says, 'As ye have therefore received Christ Jesus the Lord, so walk ye in him: rooted and built up in him, and stablished in the faith, as ye have been taught, abounding therein with thanksgiving.' True church members receive Christ personally as Prophet, Priest and King (for that is what 'Christ' means). We receive Christ by Spirit-given faith (John 1:12). This faith is active trust; it rests upon God in Christ for salvation. William Ames (1576–1633) wrote: 'Faith is the resting of the heart on God ... We believe through Christ in God.'[5] Paul tells us that we must continue as we have begun; we must go on trusting in, resting on, and looking to Christ.

A church member would be disturbed if he discovered his name was missing from the church membership directory. How much more should we be concerned that our names are written in the Book of the Lamb! Do not assume you are a believer because of a response you made or something you experienced years ago. Ask yourself: 'Am I trusting in Jesus Christ alone to make me right with God? Is he my only hope for eternal life, or am I trusting that the sincerity of my heart or my good works will open heaven's gates for me?'

Making diligent use of the sacraments

I am not suggesting that baptism and the Lord's Supper have the inherent power to save. Trusting in the sacraments for your salvation is idolatry. In its historic Reformed usage, *sacrament* means a public sign and seal of the covenant between God and man. Sacraments are also called 'ordinances', for Christ ordained their use for the worship of his people. They are a means of grace, the Word made visible.

We neglect the sacraments to our spiritual harm. Some people in evangelical churches view the sacraments only as empty rituals because God's people have the indwelling of the Holy Spirit. But are we more spiritual than Jesus, who gives us the Holy Spirit? Christ commands us in the Great Commission to baptize (Matt. 28:18-20). He also tells us to celebrate the Lord's Supper in remembrance of him (Luke 22:19). So sacraments are not meaningless rituals. They express our faith in Christ and are used by the Spirit to confirm and deepen our faith. They publicly bind believers together as one church (1 Cor. 10:17; Eph. 4:5). Living, vital membership in Christ's church obliges us to publicly receive holy baptism and partake of the Lord's Supper, trusting that, as Christ's ordinances, they are means by which he strengthens faith in our hearts and lives.

Practical obedience to Christ

In John 14:15, Jesus says, 'If ye love me, keep my commandments.' He later adds: 'He that hath my commandments, and keepeth them … loveth me: and he that loveth me shall be loved of my Father, and I will love him, and will manifest myself to him' (v. 21). Obedience is the best expression of love for Christ. Loving obedience to Christ is also the way to experience more of the love of Christ. According to his promise, he will show us more of himself. Obedience is not mere rule-keeping; it is the expression or fruit of a faith relationship with Christ, as 'faith worketh by love'.

Thomas Boston (1676–1732) was a champion for the gospel of free grace among the people of Scotland. Yet he reminded us that if Christ is our Head, we will want to keep his commandments.

Speaking of the relationship between Christ and his people, Boston said,

Jesus Christ, the head of the covenant, is their head with their own consent. With heart and good-will they have taken him for their head, for all the purposes of the covenant... And they have taken him as their head for government, as well as their head for nourishment and support. They have delivered up themselves unto him, to be ruled by him, as well as to be saved by him; to be governed by his laws, and not by their own lusts, as well as to be saved by his grace, and not by their own works.[6]

Receiving Christ's Word is the first mark of a faithful church member. Union with Christ's person is the second mark, for Christ is the Head of the body. From our living Head comes all our spiritual life, and to him rise all our hopes and desires. Let us cling to him in personal faith, celebrate him in the public sacraments of the church, and follow him in practical obedience.

BIBLE STUDY QUESTIONS

1. *Personally trusting in Christ*: Read Colossians 2:6-7. How does a person receive Christ? (See John 1:12.) According to the text in Colossians, how does a person walk in Christ? How is a living faith in Christ like roots to a tree or a foundation to a building?

2. *Making diligent use of the sacraments*: Read Matthew 26:26-30; 28:18-20. What two sacraments or ordinances did Christ require of his disciples? According to these Scriptures, how does baptism express our fidelity to Christ? How does the Lord's Supper?

3. *Practical obedience to Christ*: Read John 14:15, 21. What will we do if we love Christ? What are Christ's commandments? What are some ways in which Christians in our time are tempted to break these commands? How can they overcome?

Mark Three:
Connected to Christ's people

The third mark of a faithful church member, according to Ephesians 4:16, is being 'fitly joined together and compacted by that which every joint supplieth'. This may also be translated, 'joined and held together by every joint with which it is equipped' (ESV). *Joint* here refers to a ligament or tendon that holds together the bones and parts of the body.[7] It indicates the strong connections God expects within the body of Christ. Tendons are not just glued to bones; they contain strong collagen fibres that penetrate into muscle and bone tissue to join them together.[8] Muscle and bone cannot be separated without damaging both of them.

When God makes us part of Christ's body, we are joined together with the other members of his body. Romans 12:5 says, 'So we, being many, are one body in Christ, and every one members one of another.' A mysterious, wonderful bond holds the Christian church together so that we affect each other in many unseen ways. If one member suffers, all suffer. If one member is flourishing in Christ's Spirit, those around him are blessed.

Being connected in the body of Christ is more than formal association. My shoe is associated with my body. It is attached to my foot for many hours a day. But it is not a member of my body; I can take it off and I won't be hurt. If you try to take off my foot, however, I would strongly object because my foot is organically joined to other members of my body. It shares the same life-blood and the same nervous system. So when the Lord tells us that we are one body and are members of one another, he is saying that the church is more than a voluntary association. Its members are interconnected and interdependent, as well as mutually responsible for and accountable to one another.

We are personally connected by love

Paul says in 1 Thessalonians 4:9-10: 'But as touching brotherly love ye need not that I write unto you: for ye yourselves are taught of God to love one another. And indeed ye do it toward all the brethren which are in all Macedonia: but we beseech you, brethren, that ye increase more and more.' Each member of Christ's body should love his brothers and sisters in the Lord, and each member should grow in love for the church.

In *Fiddler on the Roof*, Tevye asks his wife, Golde: 'Do you love me?' Golde is startled by the question, saying, 'For twenty-five years I've washed your clothes, cooked your meals, cleaned your house, given you children, milked the cow. After twenty-five years, why talk about love?'

But Tevye persists, asking: 'Do you *love* me?'

When we think about being faithful church members, we often think of lists of things to do, such as set up tables and chairs, teach Bible lessons, prepare meals, play music, and attend meetings. But after completing such to-do lists, the church of Jesus Christ still asks: 'Do you *love* me?' This love demands a personal connection between us and Christ, and between all members in Christ. Such love, like faith, will of course still show itself in real terms (James 2:15-16). We will pray for and with each other, rejoice and weep with each other in times of joy and sorrow, forgive each other sincerely and completely for confessed wrongdoings, and serve each other with genuine love.

We publicly confess our faith

Jesus asks his disciples: 'Whom say ye that I am?' Peter responds: 'Thou art the Christ, the Son of the living God' (Matt. 16:15-16). Jesus then warns us that if we do not confess him to other people, he will refuse to acknowledge us on Judgement Day (Matt. 10:32-33). The identity of the church and the identity of the Christian are both closely tied to confessing Christ openly before the world.

Immediately after Peter's confession, Jesus declares: 'I will build my church' (Matt. 16:18). Earl Blackburn writes: 'The first responsibility of church membership is loyalty to the church. By loyalty to the church, I mean fidelity to the teachings of the church so far as they are loyal to the Word of God... It is only right, then, for a church to ask someone who desires to be a member to be loyal to its doctrinal position as defined in its statement or confession of faith.' Blackburn concludes that a personal confession of faith is required for church membership.[9]

We practise hospitality

Personal love and public confession become practical in hospitality. 1 Peter 4:9 counsels: 'Use hospitality one to another without grudging.' The church aims to be a family, and nothing characterizes a family as much as maintaining fellowship and eating meals together. Extending hospitality to others in the church, however, is far more than sharing food; it is sharing love and life, especially with those who may otherwise be deprived of it. The church needs to practise such hospitality.

Alexander Strauch writes about a woman who attended a church more than an hour's drive from her home. Every Sunday after morning worship, she would eat a lunch by herself, then go to a park or library until it was time to go to the evening service. She did this for four years. Not one family in the church invited her to their home. On her last Sunday at that church, an elderly woman invited her to her house.[10]

Friendly handshakes at the church door can only go so far; true relationships require spending time together. What blessings hospitality offers, not only to single people who are drawn into a circle of love, but also to your children, who have the opportunity to interact with missionaries, visiting preachers, and other adults in the church. When you extend hospitality, unbelievers will see firsthand real godliness in a Christian home. Young believers will learn from mature Christians. Needs will surface, and prayers can be lifted up for God's help in meeting those needs. Make your love for the church practical by practising hospitality.

In addition to hospitality, we have the further duty to promote the good of our fellow believers by putting our gifts and resources to work on their behalf, assisting them in things that pertain both to this life and the next. Help someone find a job or make repairs on his house or car; offer encouragement and accountability to those who struggle with temptation or are just beginning to find their way in Bible study or personal prayer.

The third mark of a faithful church member is connecting with Christ's people. The stronger the tendons and ligaments which hold together a body are, the stronger the body will be. Likewise, the strength of the church depends upon the strength of our friendships.

BIBLE STUDY QUESTIONS

1. *We are personally connected by love*: Read 1 Thessalonians 4:9-10. According to verse 9, why was Paul confident that true Christians love each other? What then was their duty given in verse 10? How can we fan the flames of our love for our brothers?

2. *We publicly confess our faith*: Read Matthew 16:15-18. Our Lord said that he would build his church on our public confession of him. How does making a confession of faith in Christ glorify him? Why is that important in joining a church?

3. *We practise hospitality:* Read 1 Peter 4:8-9. What is hospitality? Why is it a necessary part of loving other Christians? Peter said, 'without grudging'. Why might we resist or resent hospitality?

MARK FOUR:
SERVING OTHERS FOR CHRIST

Ephesians 4:16 describes the next mark of a healthy church as the 'effectual working in the measure of every part'. Every part of the church must do its job. Amazingly, we experience the Trinity through the work of every member of Christ's body. 1 Corinthians 12:4-7 says, 'Now there are diversities of gifts, but the same Spirit. And there are differences of administrations, but the same Lord. And there are diversities of operations, but it is the same God which worketh all in all. But the manifestation of the Spirit is given to every man to profit withal.' We all have different gifts, and we all need each other. Some people are gifted in helping the hurting; others are good at teaching. One Christian can give much money to help the poor and spread the gospel. Another is anointed with the spirit of prayer. Each member has a role to play in the advancement of God's kingdom. To be the body of Christ, we must be Christ's hands and feet on earth and cooperate with each other in the Holy Spirit to accomplish the Father's will.

We personally serve with zeal

Serving Christ must arise from the zeal of our hearts. Paul exhorts us in Romans 12:1 to present our bodies as living sacrifices to the Lord because of his mercies to us. The sacrifice of Christ's cross should propel us to sacrifice ourselves to do his will. Paul says shortly after that verse that this living sacrifice takes shape according to a believer's particular gifts (vv. 3-8).

Later in the same chapter, the apostle also warns us against laziness in serving the Lord (v. 11). We must be fervent in serving him. *Fervent* literally means burning hot, like water heated to boiling or metal heated to the point of glowing. Are you burning hot for the Lord? If you are zealous, you don't need a title or personal invitation to serve at a meeting or ministry. This does not mean you should thrust yourself into positions of leadership or teaching. Rather, you should be zealous to serve others, but not to draw attention to yourself. You can offer to happily take on the difficult and mundane jobs of the church for Jesus Christ's sake.

We publicly witness for Christ

In Ephesians 4:15, Paul says we should speak the truth in love. In this context *truth* is the knowledge of the Son of God (v. 13), or Bible doctrine (v. 14). Your neighbours, co-workers, friends and family members might not come to your church to listen to a preacher, but you can be their gospel friend by speaking a good word for Jesus in your backyard, in the lunch room, or in an airplane. The gospel is so simple that even a child can explain it, and so deep that we will spend eternity trying to fathom it. At its heart the gospel is the good news that God saves sinners through his Son by Spirit-worked faith.

Paul offers a brief sketch of the gospel in 1 Corinthians 15:3-5: 'For I delivered unto you first of all that which I also received, how that Christ died for our sins according to the scriptures; and that he was buried, and that he rose again the third day according to the scriptures: and that he was seen.' With that good news comes Christ's call to repent and believe the gospel (Mark 1:15). Be confident that the gospel *is* the power of God for salvation. Behind its words stands the infinite power of God and the finished work of Christ. When you speak the gospel, you are unleashing a lion! It is God's instrument on earth to advance his kingdom. So seek first his kingdom by being a public witness for Christ.

We practise good stewardship

We make our commitment to Christ's cause practical by giving money. Jesus says in Matthew 6:19-21, 'Lay not up for yourselves treasures upon earth, where moth and rust doth corrupt, and where thieves break through and steal: but lay up for yourselves treasures in heaven, where neither moth nor rust doth corrupt, and where thieves do not break through nor steal: for where your treasure is, there will your heart be also.' Our money is a temporary gift to us, like Monopoly money which is useless when the game is over. Our life is also over quickly. A wise church member gives as much money as he can to advance the kingdom of Jesus Christ. After tithing to your local church, give to missionaries and ministries that are spreading the gospel. How delighted God is when his children give for the sake of his kingdom!

The fourth mark of a faithful church member is serving others in Christ's name, and for Christ's sake.

May God enable us to be servants of the church, like the Christians Paul names in Romans 16: Phoebe ('a succourer of many'), Priscilla and Aquila ('who have for my life laid down their own necks'), Mary ('who bestowed much labour upon us'), Urbane ('our helper in Christ'), Timothy ('my workfellow'), and many others.

BIBLE STUDY QUESTIONS

1. *We personally serve with zeal*: Read Romans 12:1-11. What are God's mercies? According to verse 1, how should we respond to God's mercies to us in Christ? What does that mean in church life (vv. 3-8)? What should be our attitude to serving (v. 11)?

2. *We publicly witness for Christ*: Read Romans 1:16. Why wasn't Paul ashamed of the gospel of Christ? Why are we sometimes ashamed to speak of it? How can we overcome that fear and become bold witnesses for Christ? (See Acts 1:8.)

3. *We practise good stewardship*: Read Matthew 6:19-21. According to Jesus, is giving our money to the kingdom a loss or a gain? Why? The minimum of giving is the tithe (Matt. 23:23). Should we desire to give as little as possible, or as much as we can?

MARK FIVE:

GROWING INTO CHRIST'S IMAGE

Christ 'maketh increase of the body unto the edifying of itself in love', Ephesians 4:16 says. God wants the body of Christ to grow in him. Ephesians 4:13 says the goal of this growth is 'unto a perfect man, unto the measure of the stature of the fulness of Christ'. Our growth will not be complete until we, the church of Jesus Christ, reflect our Lord in his splendid holiness and righteousness. What a glorious destiny we have, to be conformed to the glorious image of God's Son!

As advanced in the faith as the apostle Paul was, he still longed to grow. His yearning for growth came from his insatiable desire for Christ. In Philippians 3:8, 13-14, he says, 'I count all things but loss for the excellency of the knowledge of Christ Jesus my Lord... Brethren, I count not myself to have apprehended: but this one thing I do, forgetting those things which are behind, and reaching forth unto those things which are before, I press toward the mark for the prize of the high calling of God in Christ Jesus.'

We are personally humble

In Ephesians 4:1-2, Paul says, 'I therefore, the prisoner of the Lord, beseech you that ye walk worthy of the vocation [or calling] wherewith ye are called, with all lowliness and meekness.' The first quality of a worthy walk with Christ is 'all lowliness', that is, humility. We were once spiritually dead in our sins and trespasses, but in his great love, God made us alive with the miraculous power of Christ's resurrection from the dead (Eph. 2:1-5). That truly makes us humble.

Jonathan Edwards (1703–1758) said gospel humility comes not only from fear of judgement, but also from 'a discovery of God's holy beauty' which breaks our heart because of our rebellion against him. By this gospel humility, we are 'brought sweetly to yield, and freely and with delight to prostrate [ourselves] at the feet of God'.[11] Scripture tells us: 'God resisteth the proud, but giveth grace unto the humble' (James 4:6; see also 1 Peter 5:5). If you want to grow in the grace of Jesus Christ, you must humble yourself before him and submit cheerfully to the church's office-bearers (Heb. 13:17; 1 Thess. 5:12-13). Alongside faith in Christ, humility before God and men is a primary qualification for spiritual growth into the image of Christ, for it is the essence of the one who humbled himself by being obedient, even unto death on the cross.

We faithfully attend prayer meetings

In addition to private intercessory prayer, we reveal our quest for spiritual growth by participating in the prayer meetings of the church. Acts 2:42 says of the first followers of Christ, 'They continued stedfastly in the apostles' doctrine and fellowship, and in the breaking of bread, and in prayers.' The early church gathered often for prayer. They prayed while waiting for the outpouring of the Holy Spirit (Acts 1:14, 24). They continued to pray together as more were added to the church and persecution arose (Acts 3:1; 4:23-31; 12:5, 12).

Charles Spurgeon (1834–1892) recognized prayer as the mark that preceded his own ministry. He wrote:

When I came to New Park Street Chapel, it was a mere handful of people to whom I first preached, yet I could never forget how earnestly they prayed. Sometimes they seemed to plead as though they could really see the Angel of the Covenant [that is, Christ] present with them, and as if they must have a blessing from him. More than once we were so awe-struck with the solemnity of the meeting that we sat silent for some moments while the Lord's Power appeared to overshadow us.[12]

God sends or withholds revival as he deems best. Yet God also answers prayer. If faithful membership in the church means anything, it means devotion to prayer and to gathering for prayer, praying for the church's pastor(s), office-bearers, families and ministries, as well as for the coming of Christ's kingdom all over the world. Christ was known as a man of prayer, and he taught his disciples to pray. In prayer, we come together in Jesus' name and Christ is present among us; we come to the Father, seeking his Spirit like hungry children asking for bread. Our good Father will not turn us away. So we should attend prayer meetings. They will transform us into Christ's image more than we know.

We engage in meditation

One practical dimension of growing in Christ is meditation. This does not mean emptying your mind of rational thought by repeating a syllable or contemplating a conundrum such as: 'What is the sound of one hand clapping?' In Christian meditation, your mind hovers over a biblical truth like a bee over a flower to draw out its sweetness. Meditation is taking time mentally and emotionally to digest what you learn from listening to and reading God's Word. Without proper digestion, you will not benefit from the nutrition you have received.

Thomas Manton (1620–1677) said, 'Faith is lean and ready to starve unless it be fed with continual meditation on the promises.'[13] Meditation is crucial for growing in Christ's image. The Book of Psalms begins:

Blessed is the man that walketh not in the counsel of the ungodly, nor standeth in the way of sinners, nor sitteth in the seat of the scornful. But his delight is in the law of the LORD; and in his law doth he meditate day and night. And he shall be like a tree planted by the rivers of water, that bringeth forth his fruit in his season; his leaf also shall not wither; and whatsoever he doeth shall prosper

(Psalm 1:1-3).

Disciplined meditation, which the Puritans described as a 'halfway house' between Scripture reading and prayer, offers numerous benefits. It helps us focus on God and view worship as a discipline. Since it involves our mind and understanding as well as our heart and affections, it works Scripture through the texture of our soul. Meditation prevents vain and sinful thoughts (Matt. 12:35) and provides inner resources from which to draw (Ps. 77:10-12). It offers directions for daily life (Prov. 6:21-22), fights temptation (Ps. 119:11, 15), gives relief in affliction (Isa. 49:15-17), benefits others (Ps. 145:7), and glorifies God (Ps. 49:3).[14]

BIBLE STUDY QUESTIONS

1. *We are personally humble*: Read 1 Peter 5:5-6. What is humility? Why should we cultivate humility? How does the gospel of Christ teach us humility? According to Peter, how will humility guide us to relate to the elders of our church?

2. *We faithfully attend prayer meetings*: Read Acts 1:14; 2:42. What did the church devote itself to? What is the connection between prayer meetings and the filling of the Spirit? (See Acts 4:23-24, 31.) Why don't many people come to prayer meetings? Do you come?

3. *We engage in meditation*: Read Psalm 1:1-3. This describes the man living in God's blessing and spiritual prosperity. From what does he separate himself? What characterizes him? What are some practical ways to meditate on the Bible?

BE FAITHFUL TO CHRIST
AND HIS BODY

Ephesians 4:10-16 shows us five marks of being a faithful member of Christ's body. A faithful member receives Christ's Word, unites with Christ's person, connects with Christ's people, serves others for Christ's sake, and grows into Christ's image. In every respect, church membership depends on the church's living Head, Jesus Christ.

Along with these marks we have included fifteen ways to exercise faithful church membership. Ask yourself the following questions to help you determine whether you are a healthy church member:

- Do I hunger for the Word?
- Do I faithfully attend worship services?
- Am I an active listener to the preached Word?
- Do I exercise faith in Christ?
- Do I partake of the sacraments?

- Does my relationship with Christ motivate me to obey God?
- Do I show love to fellow church members?
- Have I made public confession of faith?
- Do I exercise hospitality?
- Does Christ and his work stir me to love and obey him?
- Am I a witness for Christ?
- Am I a good steward of the gifts God grants me?
- Do I exemplify humility?
- Do I pray and attend prayer meetings regularly?
- Do I engage in the practice of meditation?

Remember that how we treat the church is how we treat Jesus, for the church is his body. Therefore, the stakes are high. How dreadful were Christ's words to Saul in Acts 9:4: 'Saul, Saul, why persecutest thou me?' If you abuse Christ's body, you abuse Christ. If you neglect Christ's body, you neglect Christ. On the other hand, what unspeakable joy the faithful servant will experience when the King of kings comes with his holy angels, sits upon his throne, calls you by name, recounts your acts of service to his people, and says, 'Inasmuch as ye have done it unto one of the least of these my brethren, ye have done it unto me' (Matt. 25:40). Strive therefore to be faithful members of the body of Christ!

Notes

1. Mark Dever, *Nine Marks of a Healthy Church* (Wheaton: Crossway, 2004), 148. Thanks to Paul Smalley for his assistance on this booklet.
2. Cited in Robert L. Dickie, *What the Bible Teaches About Worship* (Darlington: Evangelical Press, 2007), 53.
3. John Calvin, *Commentary on a Harmony of the Evangelists, Matthew, Mark, and Luke*, trans. William Pringle (reprint, Grand Rapids: Baker, 1996), 3:129.
4. Thomas Watson, *Heaven Taken by Storm,* ed. Joel R. Beeke (Pittsburgh: Soli Deo Gloria, 1992), 16-18.
5. William Ames, *The Marrow of Theology,* trans. John D. Eusden (Grand Rapids: Baker, 1968), 80-81 (I.iii.1, 8).
6. Thomas Boston, *A View of the Covenant of Grace* (Choteau: Old Paths-Gospel Press, n.d.), 197.
7. Greek *haphe*. It is 'a medical technical term for what binds the parts of the body together; ligament, sinew' (Friberg Lexicon #4169; see also Louw-Nida §8.60).

'[I]t is employed in this way in Aristotle for the connections between parts of the body' (Andrew T. Lincoln, *Ephesians* [Dallas: Word, 1990], 262).

8. 'Collagen fibers from within the muscle organ are continuous with those of the tendon. A tendon inserts into bone at an enthesis where the collagen fibers are mineralized and integrated into bone tissue.' 'Tendon', http://en.wikipedia.org/w/index.php?title=Tendon&oldid=168089657 (accessed 10-30-07).

9. Earl M. Blackburn, *Jesus Loves the Church and So Should You* (Birmingham: Solid Ground Christian Books, 2010), 108, 121.

10. Alexander Strauch, *The Hospitality Commands* (Colorado Springs: Lewis & Roth, 1993), 5.

11. *The Works of Jonathan Edwards, Volume 2, Religious Affections*, ed. John E. Smith (New Haven: Yale University Press, 1959), 312 [III.6].

12. Lewis Drummond, *Spurgeon: Prince of Preachers* (Grand Rapids: Kregel, 1992), 270-271.

13. *The Complete Works of Thomas Manton* (London: James Nisbet, 1874), 17:270.

14. Joel R. Beeke, 'The Puritan Practice of Meditation', in *Puritan Reformed Spirituality* (Dârlington, U.K.: Evangelical Press, 2006), 73-100.